Little Animals

written by Pam Holden

This frog is little.

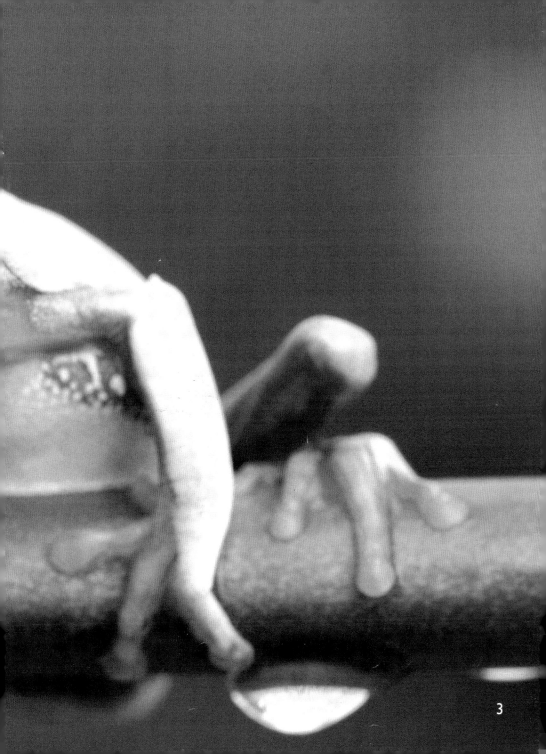

This bird is little.

This mouse is little.

This mouse is little.

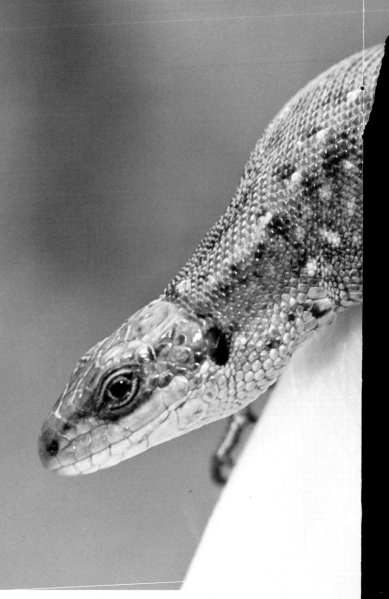

This lizard is little.

8

This caterpillar is little.

This goldfish is little.

This butterfly is little.

This bee is little.
Zzzzzz!